In this series –

RUMI READINGS
FOR
SELF-HEALING

RUMI READINGS
FOR
SELF-HEALING

JALALUDDIN RUMI

The Scheherazade Foundation

The Scheherazade Foundation CIC
85 Great Portland Street
London
W1W 7LT
United Kingdom
www.SF.Charity
info@SF.Charity

First published by The Scheherazade Foundation CIC, 2025

RUMI READINGS FOR SELF-HEALING

© The Scheherazade Foundation

A CIP catalogue record for this title is available from the British Library.

ISBN 978-1-915311-80-1

Introduction

Jalaluddin Rumi was born in Balkh, Afghanistan, in the year 1207, and died in Konya, Turkey, in 1273.

During the sixty-six years spanning this pair of dates, he produced a range of extraordinary work in Persian which, today, is classed as 'Sufi Mysticism'.

In the seven and a half centuries since his death, Rumi's corpus, which includes *The Masnavi* and *Fihi Ma Fihi*, has been circulated widely across the Near East, the Arab world, and Central Asia.

Generations of students continue to commit selections of the 60,000 verses to heart, and allow Rumi's way of thought to permeate through all areas of their lives.

Although Orientalists venturing eastward from Europe in the 1700s occasionally made note of Sufi Mysticism, they tended to witness it through the more theatrical frills – such as 'whirling dervishes' – rather than through a deep appreciation of the texts.

It wasn't until the close of the nineteenth century that the first wholescale translations of Rumi's written work began to appear in Europe.

Even then, they remained very much the purview of a few academics, whose translations were – even for the time – laden with indescribably floral and cumbersome prose.

Although in the Occident, students would find themselves scrutinizing Rumi's corpus, it wasn't until more recently that accessible appreciations of his work became available.

A few years before his death, I asked my father – the Sufi scholar and thinker Idries Shah – for his thoughts on Rumi's legacy in the West.

Sitting in his favourite chair, a porcelain cup of green tea in hand, he looked at me hard.

'I never cease to be amazed,' he said.

'Amazed by what?'

'By the way people don't take what's perfectly packaged, and ready and waiting for them, but rather obsess with something else.'

'With what?'

'With endless and nonsensical trimmings, trappings, and paraphernalia.'

My father sipped his tea.

After a moment of silent thought, he continued:

'Read Rumi in the original Persian,' he said, 'and so delicate are the verses that you have tears rolling down your cheeks. Yet here in the West, it's served up as something submerged in a thick, glutinous gravy, so much so that its utterly inedible.'

I reminded my father that a series of publications had recently found their way to press – publications that presented Rumi's couplets in an utterly new way.

Stripped bare of what my father had referred to as 'gravy', they were light.

Indeed, they were lighter than light.

My father rolled his eyes at the thought.

'In any other place, and at any other time,' he said, 'people would be up in arms. Or, if they weren't, they'd be laughing until their sides split. Imagine it – Western poets with absolutely no knowledge of the original Persian text touting new, bestselling editions of Rumi's work! It's what we call "The Soup of the Soup of the Soup".'

In the years since my father's death, Occidental society has been flooded with all things Rumi.

Couplets ascribed to him are read solemnly at weddings across the United States, Europe, and beyond.

Wisdom drawn from his poetry is tattooed daily over the backs and limbs of Hollywood A-listers.

But the precious words uttered at weddings, tattooed into skin, and quoted in abundance, hold little or no bearing to the original verses of Jalaluddin Rumi.

So, there it is…

The great Sufi Master's wisdom available:

(a) in a form that's unreadable because it's all covered in glutinous gravy, or

(b) in another form that's completely distorted – the Soup of the Soup of the Soup.

One thing that *is* evident is that the West can benefit enormously from a clean, clear rendition of Rumi's thinking – as the East has done over the last seven hundred years.

For this reason, we have commissioned entirely new translations, gleaned in particular from *The Masnavi*. Selected and translated by native Persian-speaking scholars, the emphasis has been on maintaining the lightness of Rumi's poetry.

In an age of relentless speed and digital overload, and so as to allow the work to be accessed by those who may benefit from it most, we have arranged a series of bite-sized morsels by way of theme.

We encourage you to do what students, scholars, and ordinary people have done across the East for centuries...

To pick a single couplet, or a handful – and to read them over and over, allowing them to seed themselves in your mind.

Little by little, having taken root, they will blossom and bear fruit.

Tahir Shah

How to Use This Book

Rumi Readings for Self-Healing

Healing is not a straight line.

It loops, it halts, it deepens, it surprises.

It is both softer and harder than we expect.

This book is not a cure – it is a companion.

Rumi Readings for Self-Healing offers one hundred passages selected from the classic works of the great Sufi master, freshly translated from the original Persian by The Scheherazade Foundation. These quotes were chosen not for their comfort alone, but for their truth. For their ability to meet you in the real places where healing begins: silence, longing, fatigue, and fierce self-honesty.

These are not therapeutic instructions.

They are mirrors, signposts, invitations.

They ask you not to become someone new – but to remember the wholeness that still lives underneath the pain.

A Book for Your Own Pace

You don't need to rush through this book.

You don't need to understand everything the first time you read it.

You don't even need to be 'ready' to begin healing.

Just open it.

Let one quote land with you. Let it echo. Let it ask a quiet question.

Sometimes that's all it takes – a single line to hold you through a difficult moment, a dark hour, a turning point.

The quotes are arranged in ten parts – touching on nurturing the spirit, soothing the mind, working through grief, unravelling inner knots, rediscovering truth, facing mortality, and listening to the soul.

You may read them in order.

Or you may skip around and trust what your body, heart, or intuition chooses.

Both are sacred.

Let the Quotes Settle In

After reading a quote, don't rush to interpret it.
Pause. Breathe.
Ask yourself:

- Where does this land in me?
- Is there pain this quote is helping name?
- What is it offering – and what might I not yet be ready to receive?

You don't need to figure it out.

Healing often happens beneath language. These words are not here to fix you – they are here to sit with you while you change.

A Practice of Noticing

Self-healing is not only about overcoming pain. It is about paying attention.

Attention to your thoughts, your reactions, your stories, your silence.

Each quote can help guide that attention inward – not as an escape, but as a return.

You may wish to journal. Ask questions. Let it prompt memories. Or just write what you're feeling, even if it has nothing to do with the quote.

Let it be a tool, not a test.

This Book Doesn't Expire

You may go days, weeks, or months without opening this book. Then one day, you may need it again.

It will still be here.

Let it live beside you on your shelf or in your bag. Let it walk with you as a quiet source of truth – steady, unjudging, available when the ache rises again.

Healing takes time.
This book respects that.

Share It Gently

Sometimes a quote will speak directly to something a friend or loved one is going through. If that happens, share it.

Let the quote speak what you cannot yet say.

Or let it simply say, 'I see you.'

Words chosen with care can carry more healing than advice ever could.

You Are Already Healing

Rumi does not write from the outside.

He writes from the centre – from within the wound, the confusion, the awakening.

He knows what it is to cry, to break, to return.

Healing is not becoming perfect.

It is becoming real again.

Rumi writes in this volume:

'Every adversary you face is actually a source of healing and solace for you. They serve as alchemists, healers, and all that you need.'

Let that remind you:

Even what challenges you may be guiding your repair.

Let this book help you remember.

Let it stay with you – not as a prescription, but as a quiet, steady companion on your path.

Part 1

Techniques for Nurturing the Spirit

1

When someone has a thorn stuck in their heel,
they carefully cross their foot over their knee
then search for it with care.
And, if it can't be removed,
they cry with pain.
If a simple barb in the foot can cause such distress,
imagine the pain of a thorn deep within the heart.
If everyone could see the heart's hidden anguish,
fewer would suffer in silence and despair.

2

Share your story,
let it heal;
speak your tale,
let wounds be real.

3

The love we experience
liberates us from the ceaseless chatter
of psychological theory,
and the challenges of love
shield us from moral dilemma.
Indeed, the pain of love
is the path to wholeness,
and the obstacles we encounter in love
outshine the tranquility of the mundane world.

4

Tears streamed down his face as sleep overcame him.
In his dream,
he saw himself older and graying.
'Oh, my king,' he said, 'be joyful,
for your desires are fulfilled.
If tomorrow brings solitude,
remember that we have already met.'

5

If you have lost your way,
imagine you are wearing tight shoes while you walk.
The vast desert may feel constricting
due to the tightness of your footwear.
Dreaming is like removing those shoes,
allowing your soul momentarily
to depart from your body.

6

If the divine is the healer,
then no ailment,
whether it be old age or a fever,
carries any shame or reproach upon you.
The body may falter,
but your spirit remains pure.
Illness is a natural part of the human experience,
not a mark of failure or unworthiness.
Instead of judgement,
focus on finding comfort and
care during challenging times.

7

A single hair out of place
can lead them to believe they have seen the moon
when they have not.
Even a small misalignment
in one aspect of ourselves
can impact our entire perspective.
Consider what happens
when all the components of our being are misaligned:
even minor imbalances
can greatly affect our perception
and experience of the world around us.

8

Every adversary you face
is actually a source of healing and solace for you.
They serve as alchemists, healers, and all that you need.
In reality, even your friends can become your enemies,
distracting you from focusing
on what truly matters:

presence.

9

Speak fondly of joyful moments,
so that they may be celebrated for years to come.
May the earth and sky rejoice together,
and may our minds, souls, and eyes be filled
with a multitude of happiness.

10

Being around joyful people
is like witnessing alchemy in action.
Where can we find the secret to their radiant gaze?

Part 2
How to Soothe the Mind With Faith

11

Let go of animosity and pride in your heart,
then confidently say, 'Thanks be to God'
and act accordingly.
If you thank God but feel reluctance inside,
it may be mere deception or habit.
Remember, God sees beyond the surface;
inwardly and outwardly, I am with you.

12

Remembering the divine is a pure act,
as purity emerges.
The impure shall depart,
with veils lifted,
and Truth will flourish.

13

When you turn to the Qur'an for guidance,
you connect with the wisdom of the prophets.
The Qur'an reflects the experiences of the prophets,
like a fish swimming in the vast, magnificent sea.
If you read it without openness,
you may miss its deeper meanings.
But by embracing it as you delve into its stories,
your soul will feel liberated from its constraints.

14

Examine this carefully,
my veiled friend,
for prayer unlocks the door to the response
of the Divine.

15

Evil behaviour was not inherent to your nature;
ingratitude is its sole offspring.
That evil is but a temporary lapse
leading to recognition and sought-after repentance.
Like Adam, whose mistake was a passing flaw,
with time, he repented.
As the essence of sin lies with Iblis,[1]
his path diverges from the precious act of repentance.

---

1   Leader of the devils, in Islamic tradition.

16

Do not harbour anger towards those consumed by hatred.
Their fate will eventually unite them
with those they despised.
Hatred originates from a dark place,
and nurturing your own anger contributes
to that darkness, conflicting with your beliefs.

17

Some tasks may seem challenging to begin with,
but the struggle often eases with time.
Even in moments of despair,
hope remains,
and beyond the darkness
there is light to guide the way.

18

The glow of the fire illuminates the believer's path,
for without its opposite
the elimination of contrasting forces is unachievable.
Fire serves as the antithesis of light
on the Day of Judgement,
fuelled by anger yet granted by divine grace.

19

The Prophet Jacob was overjoyed to see Joseph's face,
a sentiment not shared by his brothers.
While Jacob cherished Joseph dearly,
his brothers, consumed by spite and envy,
conspired against him,
casting him into a well of imprisonment.

20

Those who find themselves imprisoned
within the tombs of their bodies
should recognize that teachers breathe life
into the souls of the heartless with their words.

Part 3
Psychological Therapy of Existence

21

The sad melody of the reed flute
echoes stories of separation.
Ripped from its reed bed,
it has borne witness to countless sighs and laments
from both men and women.
Longing to unveil its own anguish of separation,
the flute yearns to express the pain of longing.

22

Once, I was like an animal,
before rising to become human.
Why, then, should, I be afraid?
When have I become diminished
when facing the prospect of death?
Once more I shall shed my human form
only to soar with the wings of angels.
And if I must seek the celestial beings,
then all shall fade away save the Divine Essence.
Once again, I shall offer myself
as sacrifice to transcend into an angelic realm.
That which defies imagination,
that is the destiny I embrace.

23

For those gripped by fear,
solace and security often follow,
offering respite to the troubled heart.
Yet what wisdom can one impart
to those untouched by fear?
They perceive no need for guidance.

24

The old man shakes,
gripped by the pain of separation.
To describe the agony of this rift
would not scratch the surface of its true depth,
lasting even unto Judgement Day.
Therefore, do not waste your breath attempting
to depict its burning intensity.
Simply utter, 'O Lord, peace, O Lord, peace.'
And let it be.

25

Hundreds of thousands have scientific knowledge,
yet remain oblivious to the depths of their own being.
They can expound upon the properties of every substance,
yet articulating their own essence eludes them,
like a donkey unable to explain itself.

26

Persist in your efforts to untangle the knot,
Seeker, for a tough knot rests upon an empty bag.
As you labour to unravel these threads, you age;
seek to unravel a different knot,
a knot tightly wound around your neck,
allowing you to discern
whether fortune or misfortune befalls you.

27

Those who yearn for the Day of Resurrection
are enraptured by the path of obedience.
They bear the weight of obedience
like a camel,
devoid of weariness, doubt, or fatigue.
Consumed by their devotion,
they remain steadfast
in their commitment to the divine.

28

The joy and satisfaction of reaching your destination
are intrinsically linked to the hardships along the way.
Upon returning home to your loved ones
after a period of absence,
the trials and tribulations of being a stranger
gradually fade away.
The sweetness of reunion
eclipses the struggles of estrangement.

29

In adherence to religious laws,
if someone steals,
their hand is removed;
likewise, if someone drinks wine,
and gets drunk,
their hand faces similar consequences.
These punishments arise from one's own free will
in committing those actions,
devoid of any divine coercion.
For coercion is not befitting of God,
who only bestows what is rightful and dispenses rewards
or punishments accordingly.

30

The Almighty guides the righteous along
the path of truth, while those who embrace falsehood
are drawn towards deception.
Just as a sweet-loving stomach yearns for sweets,
and a sour stomach rejects vinegar.

Part 4

Positive Psychology

31

Doctors may discern a patient's condition
through a pulse and other physical signs,
yet spiritual healers perceive far beyond
with the depths of their hearts.
Gifted with profound spiritual insight,
they possess a unique ability to discern the unseen.

32

It may appear that you are perceiving two moons,
but this is an illusion.
Focus your gaze on the moonlight,
and you will see only one moon,
without deception.
Keep your thoughts clear and uncomplicated,
avoiding skewed perspectives,
for such thinking is like a beam of light upon a pearl.

33

Partial understanding can breed illusion
and presumption, where knowledge shrouded
in darkness begets confusion.
Even a small step forward
may be navigated safely by one with insight;
yet when faced with towering obstacles,
however narrow, fear and anxiety may lead astray.
Falling into the abyss of delusional fear,
it is better to perceive the illusions that ensnare us:
fear born from delusion, delusion from our senses,
blurring the lines between reality and pretense.
At times, the grip of delusion expands,
robbing reason, leaving the mind aghast.
Opportunities arise to reveal the unseen as seen,
mislabelling falsehoods as Truth.
Thus, the soul, bereft of trust in mind and heart,
languishes in solitude,
consumed by anguish, and left behind.

34

God, the all-knowing Creator,
sculpted man from clay,
endowing Adam with a distinct form
that unveiled the mysteries woven into Destiny
and the spiritual realm.
Throughout his timeless voyage,
Adam gleaned wisdom from his comprehension
of divine names and attributes.

35

Lacking of understanding of his own worth
and spiritual merit,
a person descended from spiritual perfection
into the flawed and superficial world.
He underestimated himself,
like a precious silk fabric
decorating itself with rags.

36

Do not let your desire for more trouble you,
  for I am the Provider and Sustainer.
The One who grants you wheat for sustenance,
  will He not also safeguard your trust?
You have become disconnected from this sustenance,
  assuming it originates elsewhere,
when it is bestowed from the heavens above.

37

He who fails to find success or salvation
should not be surprised,
save on exceptional occasions.
For some sow but do not reap,
while others yield pearls without shells.
Darkness he selects for these two,
thus darkness pervades his heart.
Despite the abundance of sunlight and moonlight
in this world,
he plunges into a well, mistaking it for Paradise.
If this is Truth, then where lies the light?
Lift your head up and see, O world!

38

To witness tears,
offer compassion to those in sorrow.
To receive mercy,
extend it to the vulnerable.

39

Dwelling on the past is futile;
its scattered remnants will never return.

40

The world is under God's authority,
and therein lies our reassurance.
This truth has become evident to all.

Part 5

Personality Traits
That Perfect the Soul

41

You are more than just your physical form,
and you have perceived this.
Break free from the confines of the body
if you catch a glimpse of the soul within.
O you who are enthralled by the machinations of the mind,
its cunning and intellect,
why do you underestimate such a precious treasure?

42

I understand what is permissible and what is not,
yet you remain uncertain about
your acceptability or relevance.
You discern between right and wrong,
yet struggle to ascertain your own correctness.
You recognize the value of every external being,
yet remain oblivious to your own worth.
This is folly.

43

If you feel drawn to the heavens,
spread your wings like a phoenix.
But if you sense your inclination towards the earth,
do not resign yourself to lamentation and despair.

44

The root of all idols lies within the Self,
constructed within us like iron and stone.
For the Self resembles iron and stone,
while the idol is like the spark ignited
when iron strikes stone.
This spark can be extinguished by the waters of repentance.
How then can iron and stone withstand water?
We are not immune to either.

45

My friend,
endure the discomfort of the sting
that you may break free from the shackles of your own Self.
For those who have liberated themselves
from the bonds of existence,
the heavens, the sun, and the moon
prostrate themselves before them.
Whoever conquers their Self,
the sun and the clouds submit to their command.

46

Perfection unveils itself
through its imperfections,
while humility mirrors the magnificence
and dignity of the Self.

47

I run until my veins throb:
fleeing from yourself is never easy.
One who escapes another may find solace,
but when separated from themself,
finds no peace at all.
I am my own foe,
yet I run, my mission forever is to rise, to rise.
Nothing brings safety
to one whose own shadow is their enemy.

48

A true criterion does not obscure its nature;
it does not masquerade as a standard,
nor does it claim to be the beacon of knowledge.
The mirror that conceals flaws serves only the negligent.
A mirror devoid of concealment cannot be hypocritical;
therefore, shun such mirrors.

49

Sound bounces back in echoes,
but true essence emanates from the burning fire.
The echo of an imitator can lead astray,
like the bearer of a genuine burden
who feels its weight, and struggles.

50

A tiny seed was planted in the soil.
From it, sprouted numerous clusters of wheat.
These grains were milled into flour,
becoming bread.
As the bread was consumed,
it provided sustenance, and enlightenment.
When this wisdom was embraced with love,
the true marvel of the farmer's labour
was revealed through the process of cultivation.

Part 6

The Soul
in the Face of Death

51

The body serves as the cradle for the soul,
like a mother carrying her child.
As a woman's pregnancy draws to a close,
anticipation builds among those around her,
wondering about the sex and appearance
of the keenly awaited newborn.
The body, in its role as vessel,
nourishes the essence of life within.

52

While the surface of an object may convey lifelessness,
within it resides a vital essence.
Despite external imperfections,
its inner core harbours a vitality that endures.

53

The majestic lion roams the earth,
pursuing power and glory.
Yet the wise lion yearns for liberation
and the ultimate end.

54

Tonight, you depart as a stranger,
bidding farewell to family and loved ones.
Yet, behold, tonight my soul returns
from exile to its rightful abode.

55

He said:

'Separation accompanies the joy of reunion.'

She replied:

'No, no, true unity is found in the union itself.'

56

The journey to the afterlife
is shrouded in mystery,
as it crosses a realm devoid of tangible landmarks.
Countless souls, linked like a chain,
depart continuously
through an imperceptible tear
in the fabric of the natural world.
Despite relentless searching,
this rift remains elusive,
yet it serves as the passage to their ultimate destination.

57

Some perceive death
as the ultimate end,
resisting the injunction against hastening their demise.
But for those who regard death
as a gateway to a higher existence,
they will eagerly welcome it
when the appointed time arrives.
Those who harbour fear of death and pursue power
should proceed carefully,
while those who anticipate resurrection
should steadfastly pursue their calling.

58

I harbour no concern for this physical vessel of mine.
I am a courageous and audacious soul.
Swords and weapons hold no terror for me;
they are as delightful as the soothing scent of basil,
which brings tranquility to the soul.
While death may evoke fear in many,
to me, it resembles a vast and exquisite garden.

59

As the baby emerges from the womb,
it signals the commencement of a new journey in life.
In this realm,
it heralds the dawn of a fresh beginning,
a blossoming anew.

60

Once, it was said that
a world devoid of death would be a utopia.
However, another countered that
perpetual life would render existence devoid
of meaning.

Part 7

Humanistic Psychology

61

The flower's radiant petals shine like armour,
but when will the fruit within reveal its true essence?
When the flower fades away,
the fruit emerges, for as the outer form decays,
the inner spirit rises.
The fruit holds deeper meaning;
the flower is merely its shape,
serving as the herald
while the fruit is its true blessing.
As the flower falls,
the fruit comes into view;
when one is lost, the other grows and increases.

62

We should not dwell on loss or empty words;
instead, let us look inward and focus on here, and now.

63

The Merciful has commanded that
each day we engage in work.
On this path, carve and strive
so that until your last breath
you do not remain idle, even for a moment.

64

The meaning is concealed even when it is in plain sight;
how can people see beyond the surface?
When it becomes distant
from both its own perspective and that of others,
it gains acclaim in the world, like a phoenix.

65

With a hint of doubt or assumption
they become sceptic and indecisive,
unable to make a clear decision or argue convincingly.

66

I, who am always at peace with this 'Father',
see this world as a Paradise.
With each passing moment
there is a new form and a new beauty,
so that the experience of the new makes
any weariness fade.

67

When we find ourselves adrift,
whether in drunkenness or madness,
it is often due to the influence of the mysterious cup-bearer
and his enchanting cup.
I humbly submit to His will,
bowing in reverence,
offering my precious soul as a willing hostage.

68

The caregiver can pause and find respite, embarking on a journey into the desert in pursuit of purpose, like a resilient camel.

69

Feasting and hospitality
devoid of sincere sentiment
are mere superficial gestures.
When we welcome guests into our midst,
we do so with genuine warmth and hospitality.
Gifts and offerings serve as tokens of our joy in their
company. Feasting becomes a conduit
through which we express our love
and affection for one another.

70

Why fuss over words
when contemplation is required?
What good do they serve?
They are like thorns on a rose bush.
I shall weave together sounds
and chatter to communicate with you,
bypassing the need for elaborate speech.

Part 8

Unveiling Inner Secrets

71

Life is simply a state of internal consciousness.
And those with greater awareness
have more power in their lives.

72

We have come to understand
that we are more than just our physical bodies;
we exist beyond the physical realm,
connected to the divine.
Truly blessed is the one
who has discovered their true essence,
for they have built an enduring sanctuary of security.

73

The wise have made mistakes on this path,

afraid of not existing,

seeking refuge in it.

Where do we find knowledge?

By abandoning knowledge?

Where do we find peace?

By abandoning peace?

Where do we find existence?

By abandoning existence?

Where do we find the apple?

By abandoning the hand?

Have you grasped it,

or has it been given to you?

Behold the unseen eye that truly sees.

74

Fire attracts fire,
Light seeks light.

75

The core of all knowledge is this:
to understand who I am in the realm of faith.
You may have grasped the fundamentals of faith,
but look within yourself
if your essence is noble.
From your beliefs,
turn inward to your own principles
that you may know your true nature,
O person of virtue.

76

I have realized that my true purpose lies in letting go,
and embracing nothingness.
And so, I have made my virtual self impermanent.

77

Let go of your lower Self
and eliminate its flaws through self-discipline
to achieve a state of contemplation.

78

The man said to the dervish:
'No one knows you here.'
The dervish replied:
'Even if no one understands my true Self,
I know who I am.
I am well-acquainted with myself.'
It would be troubling if the situation were reversed,
And I was the one suffering and in pain.
Then he would be the one who sees,
and I would be the blind one.

79

When pain brings you grief,
do not point a finger at others.
Instead, look within and take responsibility.
You have been unkind to those around you
while becoming a prisoner to your own controlling
impulses. Your true enemy is yourself;
you nurture its sweetness,
yet outwardly blame everyone else.

80

It is just one dog,
yet it takes countless paths.
Whoever enters it,
becomes part of it.
Whoever has calmed you,
knows where it resides.
The demon is hidden beneath the surface.

Part 9
Educational Psychology

81

If you flee in search of comfort,
trouble will still find you on the other side.

82

Do not point a finger at others for your own mistakes.
Embrace the wisdom and understanding that this brings.
Do not be too hard on yourself:
you have already sown those seeds.
Make peace with God's retribution and justice.
Suffering often stems from our own wrongdoing:
recognize the evil in your actions, not just in fate.

83

The kindness of milk and honey mirrors
the essence of the heart.
All happiness originates from within the heart.

84

I came here seeking a dinar,
but the moment I arrived
I was captivated by the sight before me.
For a simple piece of bread,
someone will hurry to the bakery,
ready to give up their very soul
when faced with the beauty of the bread.

85

A king's true power lies not in treasuries or armies,
but in his inherent kingly nature.
His kingship is eternal,
like the radiance and grandeur of the faith of a *Hanif*.[2]

---

2   A pre-Islamic Arabian monotheist.

86

The peacocks of the soul:

prophets and saints.

They told a jackdaw pretending to be a peacock:

'You show off in the garden.'

He replied:

'No, I have not yet been to the wild.

How, then, can I describe the sound from Mecca?'

They said:

'You sing like a peacock.'

He answered: 'No.'

They said:

'Then you are not a peacock.'

87

I am sharing this difficult message with you,
so that we may explore the depths of this bitter feeling.

88

Every mind has a hidden, manipulative ruler
that can sway anyone with a specific plan.
The rising sun and its light
are also bound by this ruler's will
(the sun, too, is subject to its hidden ruler's control).
If the subconscious mind
casts even a partial spell on the Self,
it can make the sky rotate in an instant.

89

If you wish to understand the profound mysteries
of the divine,
you must not let the temptations of desire,
whim, and carelessness fill the ear of your soul.
Do not wander from the path of Truth,
lest your mind become lost in confusion and doubt.
Keep your focus sharp,
and you may uncover the secrets of the Almighty.

90

If you are unaware of your own wounds,
because you have hurt others,
it is your ignorance of your own wounds and bad habits
that causes suffering and loss for both you and others.

Part 10

The Enquirer of the Soul

91

If the inner light of the beloved
is not both in front of me and behind me,
how can I find my way with this limited understanding?
Without the guiding light of the beloved,
navigating my path becomes a challenge.
I feel lost without the presence of their illuminating essence
to light the way ahead.

92

If there was no option,
what is this feeling of shame?
And what is this regret,
embarrassment, and sadness?

93

I am not sure why I chose to express those thoughts.
The raw and unfiltered nature of my words
left me feeling powerless and consumed
by an internal flame.

94

O son,
you must break free from the constraints that bind you.
How long will you remain captive
to material possessions and wealth?

95

Trapped in the dilemma of whether to follow
his instructions or go against them,
unsure of the right course of action.

96

He went there when you discovered what had happened.
You fabricated a deception and hurt us.

97

Disregarding the difference between bitterness
and sweetness
is crucial for ascending from the unity of the rose garden.
Until you can recognize and accept this distinction,
it will be impossible for you to reach a higher state of being.

98

What pleasure persisted even after it became unpleasant?
What canopy remained unfurled beneath which roof?

99

If the servant truly distances themself from wrongful
action, how do you differentiate
when you act wrongly alongside the wrongdoer?

100

Is this how friends show their loyalty?
I am stuck in this prison while you are out in the garden.

Finis